Machines at Work
Ambulances

by Cari Meister

Bullfrog Books

Ideas for Parents and Teachers

Bullfrog Books let children practice reading informational text at the earliest reading levels. Repetition, familiar words, and photo labels support early readers.

Before Reading

• Discuss the cover photo. What does it tell them?

• Look at the picture glossary together. Read and discuss the words.

Read the Book

• "Walk" through the book and look at the photos. Let the child ask questions. Point out the photo labels.

• Read the book to the child, or have him or her read independently.

After Reading

• Prompt the child to think more. Ask: Have you ever seen an ambulance? Have you ever heard one? Do you know anyone who's ever ridden in one?

Bullfrog Books are published by Jump!
5357 Penn Avenue South
Minneapolis, MN 55419
www.jumplibrary.com

Library of Congress Cataloging-in-Publication Data

Names: Meister, Cari, author.
Title: Ambulances / by Cari Meister.
Other titles: Bullfrog books. Machines at work.
Description: Minneapolis, MN: Jump!, Inc., 2017.
© 2017 | Series: Machines at work | "Bullfrog Books."
Audience: Ages 5–8. | Audience: K to grade 3.
Includes bibliographical references and index.
Identifiers: LCCN 2016002942 (print)
LCCN 2016011618 (ebook)
ISBN 9781620313657 (hardcover: alk. paper)
ISBN 9781620314838 (paperback)
ISBN 9781624964121 (ebook)
Subjects: LCSH: Ambulances—Juvenile literature.
Classification: LCC TL235.8 .M45 2016 (print)
LCC TL235.8 (ebook) | DDC 629.222/34—dc23
LC record available at http://lccn.loc.gov/2016002942

Editor: Jenny Fretland VanVoorst
Series Designer: Ellen Huber
Book Designer: Leah Sanders
Photo Researcher: Leah Sanders, Amy Gensmer

Photo Credits: All photos by Shutterstock except: Alamy, 4, 13, 16–17; Getty, 6–7, 19, 23bl; iStock, 20–21; Rob Wilson/Shutterstock.com, 1; Thinkstock, 8–9, 10–11, 23tl.

Printed in the United States of America at Corporate Graphics in North Mankato, Minnesota.

Table of Contents

An Ambulance at Work

Ring! Ring!
A call comes in.

Oh, no! A man is hurt.
He needs an ambulance.

Two workers get in.
They will help the man.
They drive the truck.

Woo! Woo!

Sirens blare.

Lights flash.

They rush
down the road.

Cars pull over.

Zoom!

The ambulance
speeds by.

Oh, no!
There is a red light.

It is OK.

They push a button.

It makes the light green.

Here is the man.

His car got hit.

His head hurts.

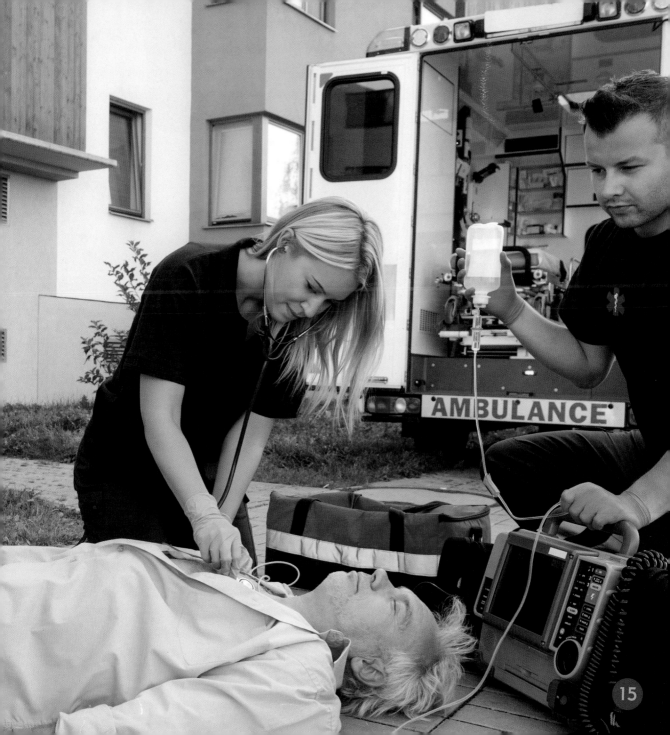

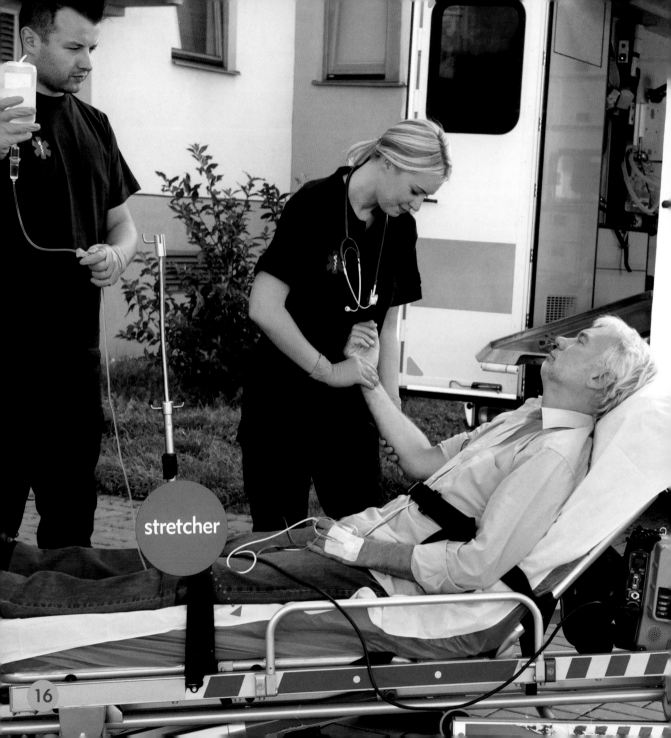

stretcher

The workers
get a stretcher.

They put him
in the truck.

Woo! Woo!
Sirens blare.
Lights flash.

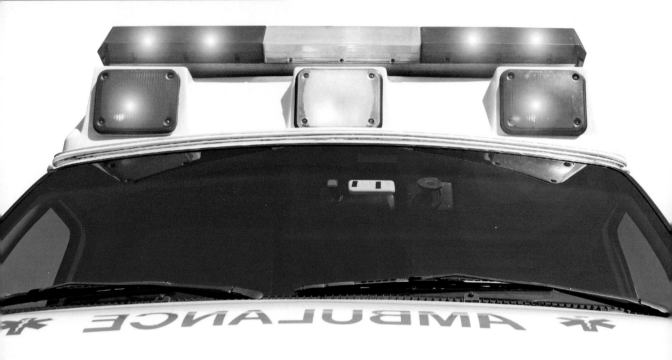

They get to the hospital fast.

AMBULANCE ENTRANCE ONLY

PARAMEDIC UNIT

Good work!

Parts of an Ambulance

decals
Words and symbols on the truck help people know it is an emergency vehicle.

lights
In emergencies, ambulance lights flash to warn other drivers the ambulance is in a rush.

cabinets
Ambulances have cabinets to store medical equipment and medicine.

engine
Ambulances have powerful diesel engines.

Picture Glossary

blare
To make
a loud sound.

red light
A traffic signal
that tells drivers
to stop.

hospital
A place to
treat sick and
hurt people.

stretcher
A bed with
wheels used
to move a sick
or hurt person.

Index

call 4	man 5, 6, 14
cars 10, 14	road 10
driving 6	sirens 9, 18
hospital 19	stretcher 17
hurt 5, 14	truck 6, 17
lights 9, 12, 13, 18	workers 6, 17

To Learn More

Learning more is as easy as 1, 2, 3.

1) Go to www.factsurfer.com

2) Enter "ambulances" into the search box.

3) Click the "Surf" button to see a list of websites.

With factsurfer.com, finding more information is just a click away.